Beyond the Bell

Unleashing the Power of Classical Conditioning

Freudian Trips

Copyright Page

Disclaimer

The views and opinions expressed in this book are those of the author(s) and do not necessarily reflect the official policy or position of any other agency, organization, employer, or company. The contents of this book are for informational and educational purposes only and are not intended to serve as professional advice, diagnosis, or treatment.

The information provided in this book is believed to be accurate and reliable as of the date of publication. However, it may include some errors or inaccuracies, and no warranty or guarantee is provided regarding the accuracy, timeliness, or applicability of the content.

Readers are encouraged to consult with professional philosophers, educators, or other qualified professionals where appropriate for personalized advice. The author(s) and publisher shall not be liable for any loss, damage, or harm caused or alleged to be caused, directly or indirectly, by the information or ideas contained, suggested, or referenced in this book.

By reading this book, the reader acknowledges and agrees that they are solely responsible for how they interpret and apply the information contained herein.

This book may also include references to other works, studies, and sources. These references are provided for further reading and exploration and do not imply endorsement or validation of the specific theories, viewpoints, or interpretations presented in those works.

Introduction: Decoding the Signals - A Journey into Classical Conditioning

Welcome to the world of classical conditioning, a realm where simple connections can unravel complex behaviors. This journey starts with a simple bell and a hungry dog, leading us to understand how we learn from the environment around us.

The Fascinating World of Classical Conditioning

Imagine hearing your favorite song on the radio and instantly being transported back to a special moment in your life, or the smell of a certain food reminding you of a family gathering. These experiences aren't just coincidental; they exemplify a powerful process shaping our responses to the world. This process is classical conditioning.

Classical conditioning is a hidden script directing much of our behavior. It's a learning process occurring when two stimuli are repeatedly paired: a neutral stimulus (like the sound of a bell) and an unconditioned stimulus (like food that naturally triggers a response). Over time, our brains learn to expect one stimulus when we encounter the other. This might sound technical, but it's a phenomenon happening in everyday life, shedding light on why we behave as we do.

Pavlov's Pioneering Experiment

The story of classical conditioning begins with Ivan Pavlov, a Russian physiologist, and his famous dogs. Pavlov wasn't initially interested in psychology; his primary focus was digestion. But while doing his studies, he discovered something fascinating: the dogs started salivating not just when they tasted food but also when they saw or even heard the lab assistant who fed them.

Pavlov's curiosity led him to a series of experiments. He combined the display of food, an unconditioned stimulus that made the dogs salivate spontaneously, with the sound of a bell, a neutral stimulus. After several pairings, the dogs started to salivate at the sound of the bell alone, even when no food was presented. This response was a learned behavior, termed a conditioned response.

The Significance in Psychology

Pavlov's discovery was groundbreaking. It revealed a fundamental way in which living beings learn, shaping the field of psychology. His work showed that behavior could be influenced by learned associations, not just by natural responses to stimuli. This insight opened new pathways in psychology, influencing how we understand human and animal behavior, treat phobias, and even approach advertising and education.

Classical conditioning goes beyond the laboratory. It's a part of our daily lives, influencing how we react to countless stimuli around us. By understanding this process, we can better comprehend our habits, emotions, and even our phobias.

As we embark on this exploration of classical conditioning, we will delve deeper into its principles, its expansion beyond Pavlov's initial experiments, and its profound impact on both psychology and our daily lives. So, let's begin this fascinating journey into the world of conditioned responses, where a simple bell's ring can unlock the mysteries of behavior and learning.

Chapter 1: The Birth of a Phenomenon - Ivan Pavlov and the Discovery That Changed Psychology

The Man Behind the Discovery: Ivan Pavlov

Before we delve into the famous experiment that revolutionized our understanding of behavior, let's turn the pages back to meet the man behind it all: Ivan Pavlov. Born in 1849 in Russia, Pavlov's journey to becoming a legendary figure in psychology was not a straightforward one. Initially setting out to become a priest like his father, Pavlov's insatiable curiosity about the workings of life steered him toward natural science and then to medicine.

Pavlov's academic path was marked by a deep dedication to understanding the body's inner workings. He was not just a keen observer but also a man of precision and patience, qualities that would later shine through in his groundbreaking work. His efforts were recognized with the Nobel Prize in Physiology or Medicine in 1904, not for his work in psychology, but for his research on digestion.

The Experiment That Started It All: Pavlov's Dogs

The experiment that would make Pavlov a household name started almost by chance. While researching dog digestion, Pavlov made an interesting discovery: the dogs started salivating in reaction to seemingly unrelated stimuli, such as the sight of the lab assistant who fed them. This observation sparked a series of experiments that would form the bedrock of classical conditioning.

Pavlov set up an experiment where he used a bell as a neutral stimulus. Initially, the bell meant nothing to the dogs. However, Pavlov consistently rang the bell before presenting the dogs with food. After several repetitions, something fascinating happened: the dogs began to salivate upon hearing the bell, even when no food was presented. The bell, which once had no effect on the dogs, had become a signal for food.

Decoding the Experiment: Key Findings and Interpretations

The beauty of Pavlov's experiment lies in its simplicity and its profound implications. Here are the key elements:

The Unconditioned Response (UR): This is the natural response to a stimulus, such as the dogs salivating when they tasted food. It's an unlearned reaction, occurring naturally.

The Unconditioned Stimulus (US): This is something that naturally and automatically triggers the UR, like the food that caused the dogs to salivate.

The Conditioned Stimulus (CS): Initially neutral, this becomes associated with the US through learning. In Pavlov's experiment, the bell became the CS.

The Conditioned Response (CR): This is the learned response to the previously neutral stimulus. The dogs salivating to the bell is an example of a CR.

Pavlov's findings were a revelation. They showed that behavior could be influenced by learned associations and not just by innate or natural responses. This understanding provided a foundational model for studying behavior, illustrating how certain responses could be conditioned, or learned, through association.

The Echoes of Pavlov's Discovery

The implications of Pavlov's work echoed far beyond his laboratory. His findings laid the groundwork for behavioral psychology and opened up new ways of understanding and influencing behavior. It showed us that much of our behavior is learned through our interactions with the environment, a concept that influences everything from education and therapy to marketing and beyond.

In this chapter, we've seen how a simple observation led to an experiment that changed our understanding of learning and behavior. As we continue, we'll explore how these principles have been expanded upon and applied, demonstrating the wide-reaching influence of Pavlov's discovery.

Chapter 2: Foundations of Classical Conditioning - The Building Blocks of Learned Behavior

In this chapter, we delve into the core of classical conditioning, unraveling its fundamental principles and concepts. Classical conditioning is like a language of the mind, a way in which we learn from the world around us. By understanding its foundations, we can better understand our behaviors, reactions, and even emotions.

Understanding Classical Conditioning: A Simple Guide

Classical conditioning is a learning process that occurs when two events are repeatedly paired together. Over time, we begin to expect one event when we encounter the other. This might sound complex, but you've likely experienced it in everyday life. For instance, if you've ever flinched at the sound of thunder because you associate it with lightning, you've experienced classical conditioning.

The Key Concepts: Stimuli and Responses

To fully grasp classical conditioning, it's important to understand a few key terms. I will reiterate them here :

Unconditioned Stimulus (US): This is something that naturally and automatically triggers a response without any learning needed. For example, when you smell your favorite food and feel hungry, the smell is the unconditioned stimulus.

Unconditioned Response (UR): This is the automatic reaction to the unconditioned stimulus. In our previous example, feeling hungry in response to the smell of food is the unconditioned response.

Conditioned Stimulus (CS): Initially, this is a neutral stimulus that doesn't cause a relevant automatic response. However, when repeatedly paired with an unconditioned stimulus, it starts to elicit a response on its own. If you hear a whistle every time before you smell your favorite food, the whistle becomes the conditioned stimulus.

Conditioned Response (CR): This is the learned response to the conditioned stimulus. Continuing with our example, if you start feeling hungry when you hear the whistle (even without the smell of food), that hunger is the conditioned response.

Navigating Early Criticisms and Acceptance

When Pavlov's findings were first introduced, they weren't accepted without skepticism. Critics argued that the process was too simplistic to explain the complexity of human and animal behavior. Some believed that behavior was driven more by internal thoughts and feelings, rather than just external stimuli and responses.

However, as more experiments were conducted and more evidence gathered, the scientific community began to see the value in Pavlov's work. It provided a clear and observable way to study behavior, paving the way for future research in psychology. The simplicity of classical conditioning became its strength, offering a foundational tool to understand and predict behavioral patterns.

Classical conditioning has since been recognized as a fundamental learning process, not just in animals, but in humans as well. It's a testament to the idea that sometimes the simplest explanations can unlock the most complex mysteries of the mind.

As we move forward, we will explore how this basic understanding of stimuli and responses has been applied in various areas, from therapy and education to marketing and beyond. The journey into the world of classical conditioning is not just a journey into the history of psychology, but also a journey into understanding ourselves and the world around us.

Chapter 3: Expanding the Horizon - Building on Pavlov's Legacy

In this chapter, we explore how the simple yet profound concept of classical conditioning, pioneered by Ivan Pavlov, sparked a wave of research and discovery. This exploration takes us beyond Pavlov's initial experiments, introducing us to other psychologists who expanded and reshaped our understanding of learning and behavior.

Beyond Pavlov: New Experiments and Insights

Pavlov's work set the stage, but it was just the beginning. Researchers around the world were inspired to conduct their experiments, testing and extending the principles of classical conditioning.

One famous example is the "Little Albert" experiment by John Watson and Rosalie Rayner. They demonstrated that emotional responses could be conditioned in humans. In their experiment, a young boy named Albert was initially unafraid of a white rat. However, Watson and Rayner paired the appearance of the rat with a loud, frightening noise. After several pairings, Albert began to cry at the sight of the rat alone, showing that fear could be a conditioned response.

These subsequent experiments revealed that classical conditioning was not just about physical responses like salivation but could also apply to emotions and behaviors.

Influential Minds: Contributions of Notable Psychologists

Several psychologists played key roles in expanding our understanding of classical conditioning:

John Watson: Often referred to as the father of behaviorism, Watson championed the idea that psychology should focus on observable behavior, not internal thoughts or feelings. His work emphasized the environment's role in shaping behavior.

B.F. Skinner: While Skinner is more closely associated with operant conditioning, his work complemented the principles of classical conditioning. He focused on how consequences shape behavior, adding another layer to our understanding of learning.

Edward Thorndike: Known for the "law of effect," Thorndike's work predated Pavlov's but laid the groundwork for behaviorism. He proposed that behaviors followed by positive outcomes are more likely to be repeated.

The Broadening Impact of Behavioral Studies

The expansion of classical conditioning moved the field of psychology into new territories. It wasn't just about dogs and bells anymore. It became a tool to understand a wide range of behaviors and even offered pathways for treatment in areas like phobia and anxiety.

Moreover, these studies sparked debates and discussions that enriched psychological theories. They challenged researchers to think about the limits and potentials of conditioning, how it interacts with innate behaviors, and its role in complex human behaviors.

As we close this chapter, we appreciate how a simple experiment with dogs led to a cascade of discoveries and debates. Pavlov's legacy in classical conditioning is not just about what he discovered, but about the doors he opened for others to explore the fascinating world of behavior and learning.

Chapter 4: The Psychology of Learning - Understanding How We Adapt and Grow

In this chapter, we dive into the fascinating world of learning through the lens of classical conditioning. We'll explore how this simple yet powerful concept helps explain many of the ways we learn and adapt to our environment. Additionally, we'll compare classical conditioning with another key learning process - operant conditioning - to provide a fuller picture of how we learn.

Classical Conditioning in Our Daily Learning

Classical conditioning is all around us. It's in the way a child learns to associate bedtime with sleep when they hear a lullaby, or how we might start feeling hungry when we see our favorite restaurant's sign. These associations are not just random; they are learned responses to the world we live in.

This type of learning is powerful because it's often subtle and happens without us actively trying to learn. It's like the mind's way of creating shortcuts, so we know how to react in certain situations. For example, if you ever got sick after eating a particular food, you might find yourself feeling nauseous at the mere sight or smell of that food in the future. That's classical conditioning at work!

Classical vs. Operant Conditioning: Understanding the Differences and Similarities

While classical conditioning is about forming associations between two stimuli, operant conditioning, introduced by B.F. Skinner, is about learning from the consequences of our behavior. In operant conditioning, behaviors are strengthened or weakened based on the rewards or punishments that follow them.

Here's an easy way to differentiate the two:

Classical Conditioning: Learning through association (e.g., Pavlov's dogs learned to associate the bell with food).

Operant Conditioning: Learning through consequences (e.g., a child learns to say 'please' because it increases the chance of getting what they want).

Despite these differences, both types of conditioning play a vital role in how we learn and adapt. They overlap in the way they shape our behavior based on our experiences.

Bringing Theory to Life: Case Studies and Examples

To bring these concepts to life, let's look at some real-world examples:

Classical Conditioning in School: Imagine a student who feels anxious every time they enter a particular classroom because they've experienced difficult tests there. The classroom (a previously neutral environment) has become associated with the stress of tests.

Operant Conditioning at Work: Consider an employee who works extra hours and is praised and rewarded by their boss. The positive reinforcement (praise and reward) increases the likelihood of the employee continuing to work extra hours.

These examples show how both classical and operant conditioning influence our everyday behaviors, from our feelings about certain places to our motivations for working harder.

Conclusion: The Tapestry of Learning

As we conclude this chapter, it becomes clear that learning is a rich tapestry woven from various processes, including classical and operant conditioning. Our experiences, whether they involve pairing a stimulus with a response or learning from the consequences of our actions, shape who we are and how we navigate the world. Understanding these processes not only gives us insight into human behavior but also empowers us to modify our own habits and responses for a better life experience.

Chapter 5: Beyond the Laboratory - Classical Conditioning in Everyday Life

In this chapter, we explore how the principles of classical conditioning, first discovered in a laboratory setting, extend far beyond to impact various aspects of our daily lives. From therapy sessions to advertising campaigns, and from classrooms to corporate training rooms, the echoes of classical conditioning are everywhere.

Classical Conditioning in Therapy: Overcoming Fears and Phobias

One of the most significant applications of classical conditioning is in the field of therapy, particularly in treating phobias. Phobias are intense, irrational fears of specific objects or situations, and they can be debilitating. But how does classical conditioning help?

Therapists often use a technique called 'systematic desensitization.' In a secure and regulated setting, a person is gradually exposed to the thing or circumstance they are afraid of while being taught relaxation techniques. For example, someone with a fear of dogs might start by looking at pictures of dogs, then watching a video, and eventually spending time with a calm dog in person, all while practicing relaxation exercises. This process helps to 'unlearn' the fear response associated with dogs and replace it with a calmer, more controlled reaction.

The Power of Advertising: Influencing Consumer Behavior

Advertising is another realm where classical conditioning plays a crucial role. Advertisers often pair their products with stimuli that evoke positive emotions. For instance, a commercial for a beach holiday might show images of sunny beaches, happy families, and relaxation—things that naturally evoke feelings of joy and peace. By repeatedly pairing these positive images with their product or brand, advertisers aim to create a positive association in the minds of consumers. Next time consumers think about a holiday, they might recall that specific brand, influenced by the positive feelings evoked by the advertisement.

Shaping Education and Training: Enhancing Learning and Development

Classical conditioning also finds its place in education and training. In educational settings, teachers often use positive reinforcement to encourage good behavior and learning. For example, praising a student for a correct answer can create a positive association with participation and learning. This reinforcement encourages students to engage more in class, enhancing their learning experience.

In corporate training, similar principles are applied. Rewards and recognition for successfully completing training modules can motivate employees to engage more in their own development, leading to more effective learning outcomes.

The Wide Reach of Classical Conditioning

As we close this chapter, it's evident that the principles of classical conditioning, discovered in a simple experiment with dogs, have far-reaching implications in our everyday lives. From helping individuals overcome their deepest fears to shaping consumer behavior and enhancing learning experiences, the impact of this psychological phenomenon is profound and pervasive.

Understanding these principles not only helps us appreciate the intricacies of human behavior but also offers practical tools for improving our own lives and the lives of those around us. In the next chapter, we will explore how classical conditioning intersects with other fields like neuroscience and artificial intelligence, further showcasing its versatility and enduring relevance.

Chapter 6: Crossing Boundaries - Classical Conditioning's Far-Reaching Impact

In this chapter, we venture beyond the traditional realms of psychology to explore how classical conditioning intersects with neuroscience, animal behavior studies, and even the burgeoning field of artificial intelligence. This journey highlights the versatility of classical conditioning principles and their influence across various disciplines.

Classical Conditioning and Neuroscience: Unraveling the Brain's Role

The fascinating interplay between classical conditioning and neuroscience sheds light on how our brains learn and adapt. Neuroscience seeks to understand the brain's inner workings, and through this lens, we can see how classical conditioning affects our neural pathways.

When a stimulus becomes associated with a particular response (like a bell with food in Pavlov's experiment), our brain is essentially 'rewiring' itself. This process involves creating new neural connections or strengthening existing ones. For example, the sound of the bell starts to activate the same areas of a dog's brain that respond to food. This neural activity explains why the dog begins to salivate at the sound of the bell alone. By studying these changes in the brain, neuroscientists can gain deeper insights into how learning and memory work.

Learning from Animal Behavior: Beyond Pavlov's Dogs

Animal behavior studies have significantly expanded our understanding of classical conditioning. While Pavlov's work with dogs laid the groundwork, researchers have since observed classical conditioning in various species, from pigeons to dolphins.

These studies reveal that classical conditioning is a universal learning process, not limited to humans or dogs. They help us understand how different species learn and adapt to their environments, which is crucial for fields like conservation biology, veterinary medicine, and animal training. For instance, understanding how birds learn to avoid toxic prey or how dolphins can be trained for complex tasks relies heavily on the principles of classical conditioning.

The New Frontier: Artificial Intelligence and Machine Learning

Perhaps one of the most exciting applications of classical conditioning is in the field of artificial intelligence (AI) and machine learning. These technologies aim to create systems that can learn and adapt like humans. Classical conditioning principles offer a blueprint for designing algorithms that can 'learn' from repeated patterns and stimuli.

In machine learning, this is similar to training a computer program to recognize certain patterns or behaviors. For example, an AI trained to recognize spam emails is exposed to large datasets of both spam and non-spam emails. Over time, the AI learns to associate specific features with spam, much like how Pavlov's dogs learned to associate the bell with food. This ability to learn from repeated experiences is at the heart of making AI more intuitive and effective.

The Boundless Influence of Classical Conditioning

As we conclude this chapter, it's clear that the principles of classical conditioning transcend the boundaries of psychology. From deepening our understanding of the brain's learning mechanisms to providing insights into animal behavior and inspiring advancements in AI, the influence of classical conditioning is both profound and far-reaching.

Understanding these wide-ranging applications not only highlights the versatility of classical conditioning principles but also offers a glimpse into the interconnected nature of knowledge and discovery. In the following chapters, we will continue to explore the ongoing legacy and future directions of classical conditioning, affirming its status as a cornerstone of psychological theory and its application in our ever-evolving world.

Chapter 7: Controversies and Ethical Considerations - Navigating the Complexities of Classical Conditioning

In this chapter, we delve into the more contentious aspects of classical conditioning, exploring the ethical implications, debates, and modern perspectives that surround this influential psychological theory. Understanding these complexities is crucial for a balanced view of classical conditioning and its role in psychology.

The Ethical Implications of Manipulation and Control

One of the central ethical concerns with classical conditioning is the idea of manipulation and control. This concept raises important questions: Is it ethical to manipulate behavior through conditioning? Where do we draw the line between helpful guidance and unethical control?

For example, consider advertising, where classical conditioning is used to create positive associations with products. While this can be seen as a harmless marketing strategy, it also raises concerns about manipulating consumer choices and creating unnecessary desires or dependencies.

In therapy, especially when treating phobias, the ethical use of classical conditioning involves consent and the welfare of the patient. It's crucial that these techniques are used responsibly, respecting the individual's autonomy and well-being.

The Debate Over Animal Experimentation in Psychology

Animal experimentation has been a topic of debate in psychology since the early days of classical conditioning experiments. Pavlov's experiments with dogs, for instance, have been criticized for their treatment of animals. The question arises: Is it ethical to use animals for psychological research, especially when it involves distress or discomfort?

This debate balances the potential benefits of research against the rights and welfare of animals. Modern perspectives often advocate for the "3Rs" - Reduction, Refinement, and Replacement. This means reducing the number of animals used, refining experiments to minimize distress, and replacing animals with alternative methods whenever possible.

Modern Perspectives on Pavlov's Methods

Today, Pavlov's methods are viewed through a lens that balances historical context with contemporary ethical standards. While his contributions to psychology are invaluable, modern researchers are more aware of the ethical complexities involved in such experiments.

Current research in classical conditioning and related fields often emphasizes humane and ethical practices. This includes greater oversight, ethical review boards, and a focus on non-invasive and non-harmful methods. There is also a growing emphasis on understanding the mental and emotional states of subjects, whether human or animal, to ensure that research is conducted responsibly and compassionately.

Ethical Responsibility in Psychological Research

As we conclude this chapter, it's evident that while classical conditioning has provided invaluable insights into behavior and learning, it also brings to light important ethical considerations. Navigating these ethical waters is crucial for the responsible advancement of psychological research.

Understanding and addressing these controversies ensures that the legacy of classical conditioning and its future developments continue to respect both human and animal welfare, aligning with our evolving societal values and ethical standards. In the next chapter, we will look at the enduring impact of classical conditioning and its evolving role in the ever-changing landscape of psychology.

Chapter 8: The Legacy and Future of Classical Conditioning - A Continuing Journey

In this final chapter, we reflect on the enduring legacy of classical conditioning, its far-reaching influence across various fields, and the emerging trends that signal its future directions. We also share insights and personal reflections from contemporary psychologists and researchers, providing a glimpse into the ongoing relevance of this foundational psychological theory.

Pavlov's Enduring Impact on Psychology and Beyond

Ivan Pavlov's discovery of classical conditioning has left an indelible mark on psychology. His work laid the foundation for behaviorism, a school of thought that emphasizes the importance of observable behavior over internal processes. But the influence of classical conditioning extends far beyond psychology.

In education, Pavlov's principles have informed teaching strategies and classroom management, emphasizing the role of positive reinforcement in learning. In the field of medicine, particularly in mental health, classical conditioning has been instrumental in developing treatments for phobias and anxiety disorders. Even in everyday life, from parenting techniques to understanding consumer behavior, the echoes of Pavlov's work are evident.

Emerging Trends and Future Directions

As we look to the future, several trends indicate the evolving landscape of classical conditioning:

Technological Integration: With advancements in technology, particularly in neuroscience, researchers can now observe brain activity in real-time during conditioning experiments. This integration of technology offers deeper insights into the neural mechanisms underlying learning and behavior.

Cross-disciplinary Approaches: Classical conditioning is increasingly being studied in conjunction with other fields like genetics, cognitive psychology, and artificial intelligence. This cross-disciplinary approach is broadening our understanding of learning processes and their applications.

Focus on Individual Differences: Modern research is paying more attention to how individual differences, such as genetic makeup, personality, and past experiences, affect the process and outcomes of classical conditioning. This personalized approach is crucial for tailoring therapies and educational strategies to individual needs.

A Journey That Continues to Unfold

As we conclude this chapter, it's clear that classical conditioning is not just a chapter in the history of psychology; it's a continuing journey. The principles that Pavlov discovered over a century ago remain vibrant and dynamic, continually adapting and expanding with new research and applications.

The legacy of classical conditioning is a testament to the enduring nature of scientific discovery. It reminds us that the quest for understanding human behavior is an evolving narrative, enriched by each new discovery and perspective. As we move forward, classical conditioning will undoubtedly continue to shape our understanding of the mind and behavior, influencing various fields and impacting lives in ways yet to be imagined.

Conclusion: Understanding the Echoes - From Pavlov's Dogs to Modern-Day Insights

As we conclude our exploration of classical conditioning, it's time to reflect on the journey from the simple yet profound experiments of Ivan Pavlov with his dogs to the diverse applications and understandings of today. This journey has not just been about a theory in psychology; it has been about uncovering a fundamental mechanism through which both humans and animals learn and interact with their environment.

The Journey from Pavlov's Experiments to Modern Applications

Our journey began with Ivan Pavlov, a Russian physiologist, who, through his work on digestive processes in dogs, stumbled upon a learning process that would become one of the pillars of psychological study. Pavlov's observation that dogs could learn to associate a neutral stimulus, like the sound of a bell, with food, and thus respond to it as they would to food, laid the groundwork for what we know as classical conditioning.

Over the years, this concept has been expanded and applied in various fields. In therapy, it has been used to understand and treat phobias and anxieties, helping people to 'unlearn' harmful associations and replace them with healthier ones. In education, it has informed teaching and learning techniques, highlighting the importance of positive associations in effective learning. In the realm of advertising and consumer behavior, it has been a tool for understanding how products can be positioned and marketed effectively.

The Ongoing Relevance of Classical Conditioning

The relevance of classical conditioning extends beyond these practical applications. It offers a window into understanding behavior at a fundamental level. It teaches us that much of our behavior, as well as that of animals, is not just a matter of conscious choice or reasoning but is often driven by associations that have been formed over time, sometimes even outside of our conscious awareness.

In the realm of animal behavior, classical conditioning helps explain a range of phenomena, from the migration patterns of birds to the behavioral training of pets and zoo animals. In humans, it provides insights into how habits are formed and maintained, how our reactions to certain stimuli are developed, and how we can change these reactions through learning.

Reflecting on the Impacts and Implications

As we reflect on the impacts and implications of classical conditioning, it becomes clear that this theory is not just a chapter in a psychology textbook; it is a living, breathing aspect of our daily lives. It underscores the importance of our experiences and our environment in shaping who we are and how we behave.

Understanding classical conditioning also encourages a sense of empathy and patience, both with ourselves and others. It reminds us that much of what we or others do is not merely a matter of choice but is deeply influenced by past experiences and learned associations.

Closing Thoughts: A Story of Continual Learning

In closing, the story of classical conditioning is one of continual learning and adaptation. It's a narrative that reminds us of the dynamic interplay between our environment and our psychological processes. As we move forward, the principles of classical conditioning will continue to evolve and influence various fields of study, from neuroscience to artificial intelligence, continuing to provide valuable insights into the complex tapestry of behavior and learning.

About Freudian Trips

Welcome to Freudian Trips, your dedicated platform for diving deep into the world of psychology. We are more than just a YouTube channel or a book publisher. We are a beacon of enlightenment, making complex psychological concepts accessible and engaging for all.

Our YouTube channel is a rich repository of psychology made simple. We take the profound and often complex ideas from the world of psychology and break them down into digestible, easy-to-understand content. From the foundational theories of Freud to the cognitive insights of Piaget, we cover a broad spectrum of psychological schools and thoughts, making psychology accessible to everyone, regardless of their background or prior knowledge.

As a book publisher, we take the same approach, transforming intricate psychological theories into comprehensible narratives. Our books are not just collections of words, but vessels of wisdom that make psychology approachable and relatable. We believe that psychology should not be confined to academic circles, but should be available to all who seek to understand the human mind and behavior.

At Freudian Trips, we believe in the power of curiosity and the pursuit of knowledge. We are here to stoke the fires of your curiosity, to guide you on your intellectual journey, and to help you navigate the fascinating world of psychology.

If you are someone who is not afraid to question, to explore, and to learn, then you are in the right place. Join us on this journey of exploration, as we make psychology easy to understand, one concept at a time.

Be sure to visit our Youtube channel at: www.freudiantrips.com/youtube

You can also visit us on the web at www.freudiantrips.com

Welcome to The Freudian Trip community. Stay curious. Stay enlightened.